How to use this book

This Year 5 Handwriting workbook is matched to the National Curriculum and is designed to improve handwriting skills.

Activities split into three levels of difficulty – **Challenge 1**, **Challenge 2** and **Challenge 3** – to help progression.

Consistent height and spacing of letters

Challenge 1

Copy the letters carefully, making sure the letters are the same height except for letter t.

b d f h k l t

Copy the sentence carefully – think about the height of your letters.

Tip   Remember, the letter t is just a little shorter than the other letters with ascenders.

Mable was talking about her favourite foods.

Challenge 2

Copy the similes, spacing your letters and words carefully.

As brittle as glass.

As bold as brass.

As old as the hills.

As flat as a flounder.

36

Copy the passage, spacing your letters and making the heights of your letters match.

November... and the long wet spell is driven away by the first of the famous Dartmoor gales. They were quite mild at first, according to John, "Only enough to take your breath away a little... you wait!"

From The Sixpenny Year by John Keir Cross

Challenge 3

Copy the verse carefully onto a separate piece of paper.

Tip   Make sure you set out the lines and space the letters correctly.

An omnibus across the bridge
    Crawls like a yellow butterfly
        And, here and there, a passer-by
Shows like a little restless midge.

From 'Symphony in Yellow' by Oscar Wilde

37

Handy **tips** are included throughout.

Starter check recaps skills already learned.

Four **Progress checks** included throughout the book for ongoing assessment and monitoring progress.

Starter check

Copy the sentences, writing in the missing words from the box below.

mistake   dismissed   distrusted

The _____ was made by the sign writer.

The boss _____ the worker because he _____ him.

Copy the sentences, adding the capital letters.

daisy lived in hull.

there was a cinema called the ritz in the centre of manchester.

12

Progress check 1

1. Copy the words.

Tip   Think about how the letters e and r should be joined to other letters.

equip   equipment
friend   leisure

2. Copy the sentences.

Peter Piper picked a peck of pickled peppers.

I saw Susie sitting in a shoeshine shop.

Where she sits, she shines,

Where she shines, she sits.

Sir Ralph the Rover was roving around the shore.

There was a rhyme that had a very hard rhythm.

30

1

Contents

ACKNOWLEDGEMENTS

Published by Collins
An imprint of HarperCollinsPublishers Ltd
1 London Bridge Street
London SE1 9GF

HarperCollinsPublishers
Macken House
39/40 Mayor Street Upper
Dublin 1
D01 C9W8
Ireland

ISBN 978-0-00-853468-4

First published 2023

10 9 8 7 6 5 4 3 2 1

P.26, 38, 'The Little Creature' by Walter de la Mare, used by permission of The Literary Trustees of Walter de la Mare and the Society of Authors as their representative; P.37, *The Sixpenny Year* by John Keir Cross © John Keir Cross. Published by Hutchinson, used by kind permission of the estate of the author.

All rights reserved. No part of this publication may be reproduced, stored in a retrieval system, or transmitted, in any form or by any means, electronic, mechanical, photocopying, recording or otherwise, without the prior permission of Collins.

British Library Cataloguing in Publication Data.

A CIP record of this book is available from the British Library.

Publishers: Fiona McGlade and Jennifer Hall
Author: Shelagh Moore
Series Editor: Dr Jane Medwell

Project Management and Editorial: Chantal Addy
Cover Design: Sarah Duxbury
Inside Concept Design: Ian Wrigley
Typesetting and Artwork: Jouve India Private Limited
Production: Emma Wood
Printed in India by Multivista Global Pvt. Ltd

MIX
Paper | Supporting responsible forestry
FSC™ C007454

This book is produced from independently certified FSC™ paper to ensure responsible forest management.

For more information visit:
www.harpercollins.co.uk/green

Guidance for parents

Handwriting at home – Year 5

Handwriting that is efficient, fluent and readable is the basis of successful writing – it allows children to compose what they want to say. Handwriting helps children learn a range of important aspects of the curriculum. Parental support can make a huge difference to a child's handwriting development – a few minutes of daily practice can make all the difference.

Year 5 priorities are to:

- practise controlling the size and relative proportions of letters
- learn to make the trickier joins between letters automatically and smoothly
- be able to write quickly, but legibly
- learn to make choices about when to 'speed up' their writing, with the inevitable trade off with neatness, but retaining legibility
- choose the correct writing tool for the job
- learn to print in lower-case and in block capitals, when appropriate
- use the names and alphabetical order of the letters to order items
- develop their own style of writing by slanting their writing.

The aim of handwriting in Year 5 is to enable children to choose the speed and style of their writing to suit the task. In this workbook we have included some longer pieces of writing to copy. This will require some additional paper, ideally lined. Copying text out onto separate paper is a difficult memory task and a challenge for even Year 5 children.

Not all children will learn with the same level of ease or at the same rate. In Year 5, children who struggle with automatic letter production or joining should practise letter movements and joins using this workbook because it will help them most as they go through school.

The first section of this workbook focuses on practising the letter joins, and the "break letters". This gives your child practice of the five main types of joins:

1. Diagonal joins to letters without ascenders (for example: *ai*)
2. Diagonal joins to letters with ascenders (for example: *ch*)
3. Horizontal joins to letters without ascenders (for example: *wa*)
4. Horizontal joins to letters with ascenders (for example: *wh*)
5. Joins to round (anti-clockwise) letters (for example: *ad*).

KS2 writers need to remember not to join break letters b, g, j, p, q, x, y, z and s because this allows them to write with maximum efficiency. The first section of this workbook asks your child to do some careful writing, with an emphasis on neatness, and some writing at speed, where neatness is not the main priority but the writing must be legible. The rest of the workbook addresses tricky joins, the relative sizing of letters, the spacing of letters and spaces between words, and puts practice of these writing issues in the context of both fast and neat writing.

The workbook also includes practice of capital letters (which never join), number formation, alphabetical order and punctuation. The workbook focuses on some of the words children need to learn in their spelling practice (from the National Curriculum list) and some grammar and punctuation issues, helping them to make the most of their practice time.

Writing tools and holding the pencil or pen

If your child has mastered all the letters, they can choose to use any writing tool. An ordinary "lead" pencil has a good combination of grip and slip and is especially suited to notes and informal texts. By Year 5, most children like to use pens and, in this case, we recommend fibre-tipped handwriting pens because they offer the best combination of friction and slip. Fibre-tipped pens are very controllable, as are ballpoint pens which use liquid ink; both are good tools to practise with. Ballpoint pens which use slippery, viscous ink are very hard to control and we would not recommend them for learners. Fountain pens are a novelty writing tool, but one which gives many learners a great deal of satisfaction and fun.

Traditionally, we expect children to hold the pencil between the thumb and index finger with the pencil supported on the middle finger. However, this is not the only successful pencil grip and the important thing is to find a grip that provides comfort, stability and control. Aim for your child to have control of the writing tool but not to grip it too hard, as this will tire their hands, arms and even their shoulders. If you think your child is gripping the pen too hard ask them to cup a ball of loosely scrunched up paper (about the diameter of a 10 pence piece) in the palm of their writing hand while they hold the pen. This helps relax the hand. It is also important for children to regularly put down the pen and give their writing hands a wriggle.

Left-handed children

Although most children are right-handed, around 10 percent of any population is left-handed. Left-handed children may like to sit on slightly higher chairs and hold the writing tool slightly further from the point, to cope with the demands of letters designed for right handers. It is harder for left-handed children to use a fountain pen neatly, because the nib may dig into the paper.

Letter formation and joins

This workbook uses letter formations which are easy for children to do correctly. It is very important that all children form letters correctly and automatically. If children learn these letter formations as a movement, they will be able to learn letter joins with little effort.

Practising handwriting and self-evaluation

With practice, your child will "feel" the correct letter movement or join, and develop fluent and even handwriting. We recommend frequent short practice sessions of 5–15 minutes, especially for children who are struggling with the formation of any letters or with developing speed. Though this does not sound like much, a few minutes a day really can make a positive difference.

When your child uses this workbook for handwriting practice, they should sit at a table and slant the page to maintain a good writing position. Left-handers slant the top of the page to the right and right-handers slant the top of the page to the left. This is good practice.

Talking with your child about their handwriting practice is very helpful and can easily be overlooked towards the end of KS2. The "progress checks" are designed for you to discuss your child's progress at handwriting and draw attention to their achievements. The "progress chart" on the last page allows your child to record how they feel about their handwriting after completing the workbook. It is always good to notice and praise efforts or improvements as it helps your child become confident and proud of their handwriting.

Warm up and revise

Copy the letters and words, making sure you join them carefully.

ag

age

thou

alright

thankfully

Copy the sentences, joining your letters carefully.

James and Josephine enjoyed their time at the fair.

They went on all the rides they could.

Afterwards, they ate lots of candy floss and got stomach ache!

Copy the haiku.

The tiger stalks you
He can't be seen in the grass
But you can fly – go!

Copy the words, making sure the size of your letters is correct.

wove

over

weaves

Copy the sentences, making sure you are spacing your words carefully.

John and his best friend travelled
a long way before they found the
treasure they were looking for.

Warm up and revise

The trees were full of birds singing.

The insects were pollinating the fruit trees and they were pleased to see there was plenty of food for all.

Use the words in the box below to write the answers to these definitions on the lines next to each.

| robin | nutcracker | glutton |

A device for cracking the shells of nuts.

Someone who eats and drinks too much.

A bird with a red breast.

Copy the sentences, adding either an exclamation mark or a full stop.

We walked to the park to meet our friends

Frank yelled, "Hello"

Suddenly, it started to rain

Copy the sentences, adding the correct punctuation marks and capital letters.

mrs smith went to the butchers to buy some meat

the toy was susies

Warm up and revise

i didnt think the story was that interesting

Copy the passage, putting in the speech marks and any other punctuation where it is needed.

Dolly was annoyed, Where are you all hiding

Her sisters kept very still they didnt want her to find them

Im coming ready or not exclaimed Dolly

did you guess they were playing hide and seek

How I feel about...	😐	🙂	😀
joining letters			
using punctuation			
copying words			

Starter check

Copy the sentences, writing in the missing words from the box below.

| mistake | dismissed | distrusted |

The _____ was made by the sign writer.

The boss _____ the worker because he _____ him.

Copy the sentences, adding the capital letters.

daisy lived in hull.

there was a cinema called the ritz in the centre of manchester.

The children ran to get their books.

raj wanted to read the first story,

"ill read first!," he yelled.

The children sat in a circle and

listened to his story. they clapped

loudly when he had finished They

had enjoyed the story, another child

stood up to read her story, "its called

beauty and the beast," she said.

selma liked this story and always

read it when she could to the group.

How I feel about...	😐	🙂	😃
copying sentences			
using capital letters			
using punctuation			

My handwriting: writing quickly and neatly

Challenge 1

Copy the words quickly and neatly. Remember to use capital letters where they are needed!

stella	the	under
are	down	by
written	ted	

Copy the sentence quickly and neatly.

My big brother made my packed lunch today.

Copy the sentence and list as quickly as you can. Time yourself.

Tip — Keep your writing legible (neat and readable).

I need to make a list for my holiday packing:

toothbrush

toothpaste

pyjamas

clothes

swimsuit

books

beach shoes.

Challenge 2

Copy the words carefully and correctly.

bargain	definite
queue	rhyme
language	carefully

Copy the words again as quickly as you can. Check that they are as good as your first try above.

bargain	definite
queue	rhyme
language	carefully

Copy the words a third time, quickly and carefully. Check that they are as good as your first try.

bargain	definite
queue	rhyme
language	carefully

Challenge 3

Copy out the poem quickly and neatly on a separate piece of paper. Time yourself.

Tip   Make sure you use the same punctuation and indents as are in the poem.

THEY went to sea in a Sieve, they did,
        In a Sieve they went to sea:
In spite of all their friends could say,
On a winter's morn, on a stormy day,
        In a Sieve they went to sea!

From 'The Jumblies' by Edward Lear

Joining to and from e

Challenge 1

Copy the words using joined handwriting.

> **Tip**   Think about how the letter **e** should connect with other letters.

even   three   elder

celery   egg   heron

Copy the sentences carefully.

Elephants eat eggs easily.

He flew freely using his equipment.

Each person held carefully onto the other person in the line.

Challenge 2

Copy the sentences.

Electric eels easily eat their prey.

Every day, elegant Ethel's earrings fell out of her ears.

Fill in each missing letter e, making sure to join it correctly. Copy the completed sentences.

B n at his dinn r.

I climb d th tr car fully.

Challenge 3

Copy the verse, making sure to set out your lines in the same way as shown.

> Tip   Make sure you join your letter es carefully.

In the house of Mr and Mrs Spouse

He and she

Would watch teevee

And never a word between them spoken

Until the day

The set was broken

From 'Teevee' by Eve Merriam

Joining to and from r

Challenge 1

These words show you how to join the letter r to and from another letter. Copy them carefully.

roll ore rhyme

bruise there rich

Copy the sentences.

Ranting Rita ran through the revolving door.

"Where is your instrument?" Ranvir asked.

Challenge 2

Copy the words carefully.

refreshing ran

rain warned

relay run

Use the words above to fill in the gaps in the passage below.

Craig _____ through the park. He had

_____ his dad he would _____

fast. Running was _____ in the

_____. He might win the _____

race for his team!

Copy the words carefully.

rehash   reverse

large   ground

harass   track

Copy the sentences.

Here is a star.

Glittering, glimmering up there.

Challenge 3

Practise joining the letter r by copying the sentences.

| Tip | Think about the letter **r** and joining it to and from the other letters correctly. |

Romulus and Remus were brothers.

Romulus, the story says, built Rome.

The River Tiber flows through Rome, which is an
ancient city.

Tourists travel to Rome.

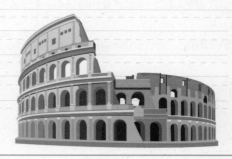

Revising key joins: diagonal joins

Challenge 1

Some letters need to use diagonal joins to join with their neighbours. Look at the words below and copy them carefully.

attached   old

occur   shoulder

identify   building

Copy the sentences.

Today has been a good day. We went walking
with friends. We saw lots of birds looking for food.

Challenge 2

Copy the words.

shoulder   muscle

hurt   bruise

Write the correct word from above into the sentences.

The other day, I _____ my _____.

I had fallen and pulled a _____.

I was left with a colourful _____.

Write a sentence of your own to finish the paragraph.

20

Copy the paragraph with the sentences in the right order, so that the passage makes sense.

The dog liked to go into muddy puddles and roll in them. "Where are you going?" asked Jess. She was curious. They all got messy! Jess put on her coat and went on the walk. "I'm going to take the dog for a walk," replied her friend.

Challenge 3

Copy the passage onto a separate piece of paper.

For the moment life was quiet and peaceful. This meant that Mrs Brennan was happy. Mr Brennan was well-rested after his latest excursion piloting a shuttle on the planet's surface and the triplets were well and truly bored.

From *Conspiracy on Mars* by Shelagh Moore

Practising ascenders and descenders

Challenge 1

Copy the words.

today   yesterday

thorough   awkward

Copy the sentences carefully.

I went to the toyshop today.

My favourite toy was the beautiful little teddy bear.

Dad and Mum also liked the bear.

Challenge 2

Copy the words.

apparent   develop

marvellous   twelfth

eleventh   thirteenth

Copy the words and definitions.

apparent — something seen or understood

marvellous — something that causes great wonder or surprise

Copy the letters.

f f f g g g h h h y y y j j j q q q

Copy the sentence.

Friendly, helpful, young and quiet are adjectives that describe a person.

Challenge 3

Copy the verse out carefully onto a separate piece of paper.

Then I'll live with my children

and bring them great joy.

To repay all I've had

from each girl and boy.

I shall draw on the walls

and scuff up the floor;

Run in and out

without closing the door.

From 'When I'm a Little Old Lady', author unknown

Placing and spacing punctuation: sentences

Challenge 1

Copy the words, putting in the capital letters where needed.

> **Tip**   Think carefully about using the correct punctuation in these challenges. Space your writing out carefully.

baby   sofia

blackpool   house

Copy the five sentences, putting in the capital letters and punctuation marks.

The man walked slowly along castle street he was tired and hungry where was the house a door opened and frank called to him the man was pleased to find his friend

Challenge 2

Copy the sentences carefully.

"Where is my puppy?" asked Gita.

"We are going on holiday," said Jessica.

The capital of Romania is Bucharest.

Copy the sentences, putting in the capital letters, commas, question marks and full stops.

Tip There are four sentences, four capital letters, one question mark and one exclamation mark.

where has my dog gone we looked in the park to
see if he was there faisal was worried as his
dog did not usually go exploring suddenly, they
heard a bark and there he was

Challenge 3

Carefully copy the information onto a separate piece of paper. Make sure you have good spacing and clear punctuation.

Pollinators are usually insects and birds. They
are very important as they help to grow our
food. Bees, hoverflies, butterflies and moths are
pollinators. They go from plant to plant and the
pollen sticks to them. Pollen is passed from plant
to plant; this helps plants to produce fruit and
vegetables for us to eat.

Writing quickly 1

Challenge 1

Copy the words as quickly as you can.

> **Tip**   When writing quickly, make sure you form your letters correctly.

Twinkum, twankum, twirlum and twitch

My great grandam — She was a Witch.

From 'The Little Creature' by Walter de la Mare

Copy the passage. Time yourself.

There are lots of flowers that need bees and

butterflies to pollinate them. Butterflies like

buddleia and some like nettles. Bees like to

collect pollen to make honey for their young.

Challenge 2

Copy each sentence carefully once. Then time yourself as you write it again quickly.

He was as agile as a monkey.

The children were busy trying to write quickly.

Chris was a fast runner and won the race.

Copy the words out quickly and carefully.

> **Tip** If you want to learn to spell tricky words, try writing and saying the letters at the same time three times over.

familiar	dictionary
queue	sincerely
familiar	dictionary
queue	sincerely
familiar	dictionary
queue	sincerely

Challenge 3

Read the poem carefully. Copy it on to a separate piece of paper as quickly as you can.

This cold grey winter afternoon

The starlings

On the television aerial

Look like sultanas on a stalk.

'Starlings' by Lucy Hosegood

27

Writing neatly 1

Challenge 1

Copy the words as neatly as you can.

immediately

curiosity

twelfth

quickly

Fill in the gaps in the passage with the words above.

Dari walked _____ along the road. It was the _____ of December. Her _____ was roused when she saw a map in a shop window. _____, she went into the shop to look at the map.

Challenge 2

Copy the phrases and put in the collective noun from the box.

| forest | choir | army | bunch |

an _____ of soldiers

a group of singers is a _____

a _____ of grapes

a _____ of trees

📖 Copy the letter as neatly as you can using joined handwriting on to a separate piece of paper.

10; The Grove
Blackpool
B010 TW5

Dear Francis,

I am writing to thank you for your kind invitation to your party. I am delighted to accept your invitation. I look forward to seeing you next week on Wednesday, 25th June.

With best wishes

From your friend

Adnan

Challenge 3

Copy the sentence and words as neatly as you can.

Some English words come from Old English whilst others originate from French, for example:

Old English	French
ox _____	beef _____
sheep _____	mutton _____
begin _____	commence _____
child _____	infant _____

1. Copy the words.

Tip — Think about how the letters **e** and **r** should be joined to other letters.

equip   equipment

friend   leisure

2. Copy the sentences.

Peter Piper picked a peck of pickled peppers.

I saw Susie sitting in a shoeshine shop.

Where she sits, she shines,

Where she shines, she sits.

Sir Ralph the Rover was roving around the shore.

There was a rhyme that had a very hard rhythm.

3. Think about diagonal joins. Copy the sentences.

The other day, I went walking with a friend. We came across a lost dog which looked very forlorn and lost. We took it to our local vet and the dog was checked out. Later, we learnt it was safe and with its owner.

4. Copy the words carefully.

attached

temperature

hindrance

neighbour

How I feel about...	😐	🙂	😃
joining diagonals			
my ascenders			
my descenders			

Progress check 1

5. Copy the sentences, adding punctuation and capital letters.

mary had a little lamb

where do I want to go on holiday

i think sofia is good at painting

yesterday we all went to the circus in blackpool

6. Copy the passage as quickly and carefully as you can.

Shardha, Rohan and Etsuka approached their mother carefully. They had decided that Shardha could do the asking; she was more likely to get their mother's permission to use the family's Mars Rover.

From *The Martian Conspiracy* by Shelagh Moore

7. Copy the verse as neatly as possible.

Tell me a story, Father, please do;

I've kissed Mama and I've said my prayers,

And I bade goodnight to the soft pussy-cat

And the little mouse that lives under the stairs.

From 'Request Number' by G.N. Sprod

How I feel about...	😐	🙂	😀
spacing punctuation			
writing quickly			

Alphabetical order

Challenge 1

Write the words in alphabetical order.

| neighbour achieve forty safety believe |

Challenge 2

Here is a grid with words in the wrong alphabetical order. Use joined handwriting to write the words in the correct alphabetical order in the wall below. The first one has been done for you.

snow		early		jumper
	winter		toboggan	
holiday		cold		hats
	day		one	

cold

Challenge 3

Copy the poem.

Tip	This comic poem uses letters of the alphabet instead of words. It has to be spoken out loud to get its meaning! Enjoy reading it out after you have copied the poem!

ABCD Goldfish?

MNO Goldfish!

OSDR Goldfish

RDR Goldfish!

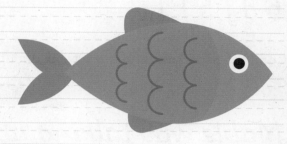

Translation:

Abbie, see da goldfish?

Them no goldfish!

Oh yes they are goldfish

Aah they are goldfish!

Consistent height and spacing of letters

Challenge 1

Copy the letters carefully, making sure the letters are the same height except for letter **t**.

b d f h k l t

Copy the sentence carefully – think about the height of your letters.

| Tip | Remember, the letter **t** is just a little shorter than the other letters with ascenders. |

Mable was talking about her favourite foods.

Challenge 2

Copy the similes, spacing your letters and words carefully.

As brittle as glass.

As bold as brass.

As old as the hills.

As flat as a flounder.

Copy the passage, spacing your letters and making the heights of your letters match.

November... and the long wet spell is driven away by the first of the famous Dartmoor gales. They were quite mild at first, according to John, "Only enough to take your breath away a little... you wait!"

From *The Sixpenny Year* by John Keir Cross

Challenge 3

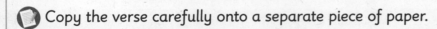 Copy the verse carefully onto a separate piece of paper.

| Tip | Make sure you set out the lines and space the letters correctly. |

An omnibus across the bridge
　　Crawls like a yellow butterfly
　　And, here and there, a passer-by
Shows like a little restless midge.

From 'Symphony in Yellow' by Oscar Wilde

Joining to and from t

Challenge 1

Copy the words.

> **Tip**   Remember, the letter **t** is slightly shorter than other tall letters.

acted	bitsy
delta	forth
pitta	stray
truth	underneath

Copy the sentences.

He acted on the stage for ten years until he retired.

Twinkum, twankum, twirlum and twitch

My great grandam – She was a Witch.

From 'The Little Creature' by Walter de la Mare

Challenge 2

Copy the words in joined writing.

at	ate
eat	eaten
grant	granted
thwart	thwarted

Copy the sentences and insert the missing words from the list.

| temperature | thorough | cold | then | doctor |

I had a _____ . The _____

gave me a _____ examination.

_____ I was told I had a _____

and had to stay in bed.

Challenge 3

Copy the tongue twisters. How quickly can you say them?

Two tadpoles trying to tease a fish got eaten in a trice.

Twisting, twirling, turning round leaves tumbling to the ground.

The tired tyrannosaurus tripped into the tree, the tree tumbled down into the sea!

Joining to and from f

Challenge 1

Copy the words. Think about the height and depth of the letter f.

Tip   Remember the letter f goes above and below the line.

familiar   fortify

effortless   confidence

Copy the sentence.

Five playful pups were fooling around in the carefully planted flowerbed.

Challenge 2

Copy the sentences carefully.

Tip   You will need to join to f with a diagonal join and from it with a horizontal join when writing some words.

Forty mums were after waterproof coats of different colours.

They were feeling full after eating lots of fruit.

Fluffy was an affable but bashful cat.

Copy the sentences and put in the missing words from the list below.

fairies	forest	mayflies	flutter

_____ are shy insects. They _____ with the _____ in the _____ glades.

Challenge 3

Write the words in the correct alphabetical order.

chiefly	bashful	faithfully	enfold	affects

Write your own sentence containing one of the words in the box above.

Revising key joins: horizontal joins

Challenge 1

Copy the words carefully. Think about how they join to each other.

| Tip | Horizontal joins go across to small letters or up to tall ones. |

variety   dictionary

rhythm   sincere

Copy the sentences.

The boys were in favour of walking to school.

Knock on the door and ask for your friend.

Challenge 2

Complete the table with words that are synonyms of the word in the first column. The first one has been done for you.

| Tip | A synonym is a word that has a similar meaning. |

| device | waver | stomach | crisis |

hesitate	waver
emergency	
gadget	
tummy	

Copy the sentences.

Someone who is adventurous might take risks.

The location of a place can often be found on a map.

Shops supply goods for people to buy.

Challenge 3

Copy the lines from a witch's recipe.

Double, double, toil and trouble;

Fire burn and cauldron bubble.

 Fillet of a fenny snake

In the cauldron boil and bake:

From *Macbeth* by William Shakespeare

Break letters: y, j, g, p

Challenge 1

Not all letters join to the next letter. These are called break letters.

Tip — Remember, letters **y**, **j**, **g** and **p** never join to the next letter.

Copy the words.

yacht   join

giraffe   pedal

Copy the sentence.

Gorillas joining the group behave very carefully.

Challenge 2

Copy the sentences.

Tip — Remember to keep your descenders straight so that your words are easy to read.

Peter jogged along the yellow path to the gate.

Help me get my pan off the shelf please.

The yellow, green and pink squares are joined
up in a pattern to make the quilt look pretty.

Copy the sentences.

Jasper got a bag of grapes from a young friend.

The seagulls on the roof are noisy, aggressive young birds.

Peter Piper found a growth of pickled yellow peppers in the adjoining garden.

Challenge 3

Write in the missing letters y, j, g or p. Copy the sentences.

My friend jo __ s every da __ so that he can keep playing hocke __ .

Mum made __ am in a __ an but she could not find any jam __ ars so she had to __ o and bu __ some.

Getting height right: capital letters

Challenge 1

Copy the alphabet using capital letters only.

A B C D E F G H I J K L M N
O P Q R S T U V W X Y Z

Copy the placenames.

London   Madrid

Paris   Nairobi

Challenge 2

Copy the sentences.

Manchester, Hull and Lincoln are all cities.

Christopher, Kostas, Jung and Kenji are all boys' names.

Leah, Jennie, Amira and Jessica are all girls' names.

Copy the sentences, putting in the capital letters.

my friend daisy wanted to go to london to see the tower of london.

rufus thought moonfleet was a base on the moon.

i thought delia and danny would like to go on a picnic to weymouth beach.

Challenge 3

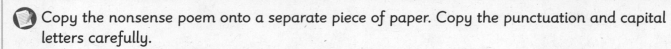 Copy the nonsense poem onto a separate piece of paper. Copy the punctuation and capital letters carefully.

Says she to me, "Was that you?"

Says I, "Who?"

Says she, "You."

Says I, "Where?"

Says she, "There."

Says she, "Then."

Says I, "No."

Says she, "Oh…"

47

Placing and spacing punctuation: commas and bullet points in single-word lists

Challenge 1

Copy the sentences.

Tip   Remember to put commas between items, places or names when you are listing them in a sentence.

Sheena, Patty, Joy and Joseph all went to the party.

Manchester City, Manchester United, Burnley and Blackpool are all football teams in North-West England.

Challenge 2

Copy the lists using bullet points. The first one has been done for you.

He bought socks, shoes, trousers and a jumper.

He bought:

• socks

• shoes

• trousers

• a jumper.

She visited London, Paris, Helsinki and Rome.

Copy the sentences, adding commas where needed to make the meaning clear.

We needed scissors paper glue and glitter for the craft activity.

Their grandpa was a tall thin happy playful man.

Challenge 3

Copy the sentences onto a separate piece of paper, putting in either commas or bullet points where needed to make the meaning clear.

Their uncle and aunt gave them coats hats gloves and scarves to wear on their walk.

The teacher told them to copy learn listen repeat.

Progress check 2

1. Write the words in the correct alphabetical order.

| hunter | bargain | stomach | cupboard | muscle |

2. Write the missing words from the box into the sentences.

| set | howl | evening | run | tried | fox | dog |

The _____ was walking along the road in the _____. He saw a _____ in the nearby field and started to _____. Both animals decided to _____. The fox _____ off to hide and the dog _____ to find him.

3. Write the words in the correct alphabetical order.

| symbol | forty | queue | rhyme | occur |

4. Copy the sentence using the correct height and spacing of letters.

My mother said I should never go out without telling her where I was going.

5. Copy the sentences, making sure the letter t is the correct height.

I lit my birthday candles and we all blew them out.

The inbox was full. I emptied it to make sure that I would get more emails.

6. Copy the sentences carefully, making sure you are joining the letter f correctly.

He was from France and had flown into Farnborough.

Fifty-five feathers were seen floating down from the sky.

How I feel about...	😐	🙂	😀
alphabetical order			
joining to and from the letter f			
joining to and from the letter t			

7. Copy the words and sentence. Make sure your horizontal joins are correct.

| Tip | Remember, some letters do not join to the letters next to them. |

windows order programme brown woodwork

The young child jogged around the playground five times.

8. Copy the sentences, putting in the capital letters.

| Tip | Think about the height of your capital letters. |

they thought liverpool had a ferry across the river mersey.

adam and ben were cousins who lived in surrey.

tonight, i am going to the bowling alley with amelia and joe.

9. Copy the lists.

They needed flour, eggs, sugar, butter and a bit of milk to make the Victoria sponge cake.

We need:

- Flour
- Eggs
- Sugar
- Butter
- Milk

How I feel about...	🙂	🙂	😃
my horizontal joins			
spacing punctuation			
punctuating lists			

Writing direct speech neatly

Challenge 1

Copy the sentences neatly, making sure you put the speech marks in correctly.

"I would like to have a drink," said Aidan.

"Would you like orange juice?" asked his mum.

"Yes please, I am feeling very thirsty," he replied.

Challenge 2

Copy the direct speech into the sentences making sure you put in the speech marks and other punctuation carefully and neatly.

Tip Remember, commas and other sentence punctuation go before you close the direct speech marks.

said Harry.

His dad smiled at him.

he said.

Copy the sentences about a boy who caught a fish.

"I've got a bite!" yelled Sid excitedly. "It's a big one, I think," he added.

His dad called to him, "Take it carefully, you don't want to lose him."

"Look, look, it's massive! Help me Dad, he's very heavy," said Sid.

Challenge 3

Copy the sentences onto a separate piece of paper, putting the speech marks in the correct places.

I'm really tired after all this walking, said Jade.

Do you think we will be there soon? she asked.

I'm feeling hungry, I hope they have tea for us, she added.

Placing and spacing punctuation: apostrophes in contractions

Challenge 1

Copy the words carefully.

Tip	The first column is the word in full, the second column is the contraction with an apostrophe to indicate the missing letters.

I am	I'm
he is	he's
she is	she's
we are	we're
you are	you're
they are	they're
where is	where's

Copy the sentence.

We're three friends – where's the other one?

Challenge 2

Copy each contraction and then write it out in full. The first one has been done for you.

wasn't	wasn't	was not
don't		
can't		
won't		
didn't		

Complete the sentences by putting in the correct contraction from the bottom of page 56.

I _____ like homework.

We _____ get the model to work properly.

They _____ break it, they are careful children.

Salem _____ go rock climbing because

he was away on holiday.

Copy the words and their contraction.

Tip   Remember, only use contractions in informal writing, such as direct speech and letters to friends.

would not, wouldn't

had not, hadn't

cannot, can't

should have, should've

Challenge 3

Copy the passage onto a separate piece of paper, putting the apostrophes in the correct places.

I think Im better than you at balancing, as you
cant stand on one leg with your eyes closed! Ive
been practising a lot. I shouldve gone to gym
classes but we couldnt because we wouldve had
to go on a day when I've got music lessons.

Alphabetical order to the second letter

Challenge 1

Copy the words, They are in alphabetical order.

amateur   available

bargain   bruise

harass   help

zebra   zone

Copy the pairs of words, putting them in the correct alphabetical order.

sent, scent

two, too

except, accept

buy, by

peace, piece

Challenge 2

Copy the shopping list, putting the items in alphabetical order.

fish, avocado, peas, bread, apples, butter, flour, pancakes, yoghurt, biscuits, yams

Here are some words describing a girl and a boy. Put them in alphabetical order on the lines below. The first ones have been done for you.

cheerful
sorrowful
bubbly
serious
pleasant
bright
grumpy
solemn
sad
caring
glum
practical

GIRL:

bright

BOY:

glum

Challenge 3

Copy the words onto a separate piece of paper. Underline the words that are in alphabetical order.

Jibber, jabber, gabble, babble

Cackle, clack and prate,

Twiddle, twaddle, mutter, stutter,

Utter, splutter, blate.

From 'What Some People Do' by Anonymous

Writing neatly 2

Challenge 1

Copy the passage neatly.

> **Tip** Think about the height and shape of the letters you are writing. Make sure your letters **u** and **v** are written correctly.

Pat's parrot Polly was ill so she took it to the vet. The vet thought that Polly needed to be able to talk to people so Pat took Polly to the local park and Polly said hello to the people in the park.

Challenge 2

Copy the words quickly and neatly. Stop after 30 seconds.

bargain exaggerate individual dictionary nuisance

Copy the sentences neatly, putting in the correct punctuation.

usually on a special occasion we have cake

steve wanted to make a gigantic sandcastle

do you think theyd run the race for us said meg

Challenge 3

Copy the poem as neatly as you can.

The song of canaries

Never varies,

And when they're moulting

They're pretty revolting.

'The Canary' by Ogden Nash

Writing notes quickly

Challenge 1

Copy the words quickly and carefully.

bullet points   details

phrases   notes

Copy the note.

| Tip | Notes are ways of reminding us of what we need to do – they help us remember things. |

To: Sean   Date: 23 March 2022   Time: 10.30am

Phone your mum for shopping list.

Challenge 2

Write down the main ideas in a bulleted list from the message below. The first one is done for you.

Hello Sean, thanks for calling back. Can you buy eggs, bacon, sausages and bread for supper please?

NOTE:

Need:

• eggs

Copy the message and then make it into a note.

Tip   Remember to only include the important information.

Alice called today, on 10th June at 10am. Could you ask Colin to meet Alice at the museum on Smart Street today, at 4 o'clock in the afternoon, for orange juice and cakes?

NOTE:

From: Date: Time:

Message:

Challenge 3

Write a note listing things to take to the beach.

63

Joining to and from k

Copy the words.

| Tip | Think about how the letter **k** joins to another letter and from another letter. |

bracket

knight

knick-knack

look

Copy the sentence carefully.

The jukebox in Alaska was playing while Kristen
was baking.

Challenge 2

Copy the sentences and fill in the gaps with the correct words.

| awkward | kicking | nickname |

Jake loved _____ his football.

It was _____ when the cooks both
brought the same cakes to the sale.

Knuckle was the _____ of the king's knight.

Write the words from the box to match the correct definitions.

kind	keepsake	reckon	weak

to add up, count

friendly, helpful, thoughtful

lacking in strength

something we value, a souvenir, reminder of something

Challenge 3

Copy the acrostic poem.

> **Tip**   Make sure you join the **k** carefully and put in all the punctuation.

Jake is kind and not

Awkward, loves kicking a ball,

Knows where the net is, it's

Exciting to see him kick back the ball!

Revising key joins: joins to and from round letters

Challenge 1

Copy the words. Think about how the round letters join to and from other letters.

according   easily

community   ignore

Copy the sentence.

We spread out the sewing evenly onto the floor
so we could see what it looked like.

Challenge 2

Copy the sentences, putting in the missing words.

| slate   snowed   broom   groaned |
| classroom   roof   ice cream |

Last night, a _____ fell off the _____.

When it _____, I thought the world
looked like it was covered in _____.

"We need a _____ to sweep the _____,"
said the teacher.

📄 Copy the instructions of how to make a collage onto a separate piece of paper.

Firstly, collect pictures and coloured paper.

You will also need scissors, glue and pencils.

Secondly, draw the outlines of the picture you

want to make onto the paper.

Thirdly, cut out the shapes from the pictures

and pieces of coloured paper you have.

Finally, stick them onto your paper to make

your picture.

Challenge 3

Write the collective nouns in the correct groups.

| pack | swarm | shoal | flock |

A _____ of bees

A _____ of sheep

A _____ of wolves

A _____ of fish

Getting the height right: i, a, l

Challenge 1

Copy the words. Make sure the heights of the letters are correct.

indeed

explanation

familiar

immediately

Copy the sentence.

Special parcels arrive and are opened immediately.

Challenge 2

Copy the words, then place them in the sentences and copy them out.

shield   failure

trials   sociable

The man tried to _____ his dog from the

other dogs at the dog _____.

People who live here are very _____.

My cake was a _____ as it tasted horrible.

Write the words from the box to match the correct definitions. The first one has been done for you.

| especially calligraphy explanation variety |

something in particular or specifically

when we are told what something means

a collection of unlike things

beautiful handwriting in a specially chosen style

Challenge 3

Copy the lines. Make sure the heights of the letters i, a, and l are correct.

All my family enjoy walking in the woods.

We collect snails in pails,

Then we lose them easily in logs.

Later, they eat leaves and enjoy the rain!

Printing and labelling

Challenge 1

There are times when we decide to print and do not join letters. Copy the printed words.

Samantha

Highway House

Copy the sentence in print.

Samantha lived in Highway House, which was
on The Lane and was a cul-de-sac.

Challenge 2

Copy the printed words to label the diagram. The first one has been done for you.

| Tip | Think about the size of your printed letters so they will fit in the space. |

head   nose   eye   chin   ear   elbow
hand   leg   knee   foot

Copy the printed words to label the flowers, bug hotel, bird box and Children's Garden sign.

sunflowers	roses	tulips	bug hotel
bird box		Children's Garden	

Challenge 3

Copy the address, remembering to put the postcode in capital letters.

7 Wild Road

Corby

London

WI4 6JR

Progress check 3

1. Copy the sentences, making sure you put the speech marks in correctly.

Jason, where's my football? asked his sister.

I'm sorry, I kicked it over the fence when I was practising, replied Jason apologetically.

Well, we'd better go and get it, replied his sister.

2. Copy the sentences, changing the underlined words into their contractions.

<u>I would</u> like to see your homework.

We went for a walk, I <u>did not</u> like the dark wood.

How are you? Here, <u>we are</u> all enjoying our holiday by the seaside.

3. Copy the words in the correct alphabetical order.

| hare | buzz | chatter | prattle | crack |
| patter | bark | hem | | |

4. Copy the nonsense poem neatly.

Order in the court

The judge is eating beans

His wife is in the bath tub

Shooting submarines

From *The Kingfisher Book of Children's Poetry*

How I feel about...	😐	🙂	😀
alphabetical order to the second letter			
using contractions			
using speech marks			

5. Copy the note quickly.

To: Natasha   Date: 7th May 2022   From: Mr Smith

Please see me in my office at 2pm.

Bring your artwork for the exhibition with you.

6. Copy the sentences, making sure all your joins and letter heights are correct.

Each and every potato must be baked well for lunch.

When are you going to eat your potato?

We need to run to the shops to buy some more.

I am partial to a baked potato.

We often have them for tea with melted cheese.

7. Print labels for each shop counter – sweet counter, bread counter and fruit counter.

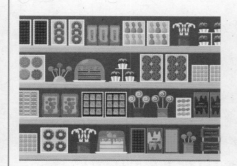

How I feel about...	😐	🙂	😃
my legible writing			
writing quick notes			
printing and labelling			

Placing and spacing punctuation: speech marks

Challenge 1

Copy the sentences.

"I would like to go swimming," said Penelope.
"Can I go tomorrow?"

"Yes, I expect you can," replied her mum, "but you will have to ask your dad if he can take you."

Challenge 2

Copy the sentences, putting in the speech marks. The first one has been done for you.

| .Tip | Remember that speech marks go around the words spoken and any punctuation. |

"Please may I go home now?" asked the patient.

There are ten spellings to learn, said the teacher.

Oh bother, said Sam, I really wanted to play football!

Faizan called to his sister, Hurry up or we'll miss the bus.

I'm hurrying, called his sister as she ran to catch him up. Wait for me will you?

Finish writing the conversation. What could Jon say to his mum? Remember to put in speech marks for direct speech.

Tip	Remember that every time a new person speaks you start on a new line.

Jon asked, "Please may I go to the park with my friends, Mum?"

"Well," replied his mum, "I think you need to finish your homework first, don't you?"

Writing quickly 2

Challenge 1

Copy the words quickly and neatly.

> **Tip**
>
> If you are right-handed, make sure the top of your page is slanted towards the left. If you are left-handed, the top of your page will be slanted towards the right. You will find this helps you to improve your writing speed.

eaten   scrambled

bruise   exaggerate

Copy the poem. Time yourself. How long did it take you to write it?

Mary had a little lamb

Its fleece was white as snow

Until it rolled into the mud

And went as dark as coal!

It took me _____ to write out the poem.

Challenge 2

Copy the following passage. Time how long it takes you to complete the task.

A messenger from the king arrived and gave a

letter to Edwin.

"Read this to me Alwin; my eyes are tired," instructed his father. Edwin found reading harder than he liked to admit to his son.

From *The Boy Who Helped a King* by Shelagh Moore

Are all your words readable? Rewrite the ones you think could be neater.

Challenge 3

Copy this list as fast as you can. Rewrite any words you are not happy with.

You need to pack:

- pyjamas
- toothbrush
- underwear
- socks
- trousers
- shoes.

Writing neatly 3

Challenge 1

Copy the addresses neatly and correctly. As it is a formal letter, your address should be on the right-hand side of the page. You write the address of the person you are sending the letter to on the left-hand side.

Holly Lodge
Holly Lane
Denby Dale
DB9 6AZ

Frank Jones
The Ark
Swindon
SW5 2DN

Challenge 2

Copy the following heading and start of the letter.

About: A complaint about a delivery.

Dear Mr Jones,

I am writing to ask you to replace my scooter.
When it was delivered there was a wheel
missing so I could not use the scooter.

 Write the rest of the letter as neatly as you can onto a separate piece of paper. You want Mr Jones to read your letter and reply to it quickly.

Tip	Think about saying how disappointed you were that your scooter was broken. Mention that you hope it will be replaced quickly. Sign it 'Yours sincerely,' as you know the name of the person you are writing to.

Challenge 3

 Read your letter carefully and correct any mistakes in punctuation and spelling. Copy it onto a separate piece of paper.

Spacing items in a list: commas and bullet points

Challenge 1

Put the commas in the sentence to separate the items in the description.

Maisie was tall she had blue eyes blonde hair and wore a ribbon in her hair.

Copy the sentence, making sure you put in the commas correctly.

Farid wanted to buy sweets drinks crisps and comics.

Challenge 2

Copy the sentence using bullet points instead of commas.

Rashid and Joe went to the beach. They took: buckets, spades, sandwiches, drinks and towels.

Copy the sentences, punctuating them with capital letters, commas and full stops.

please may i have a packet of biscuits a bottle of
apple juice an ice cream and a bag to put them in

the man ran along the beach he wanted
to catch up with sajid jane isabel and john

Challenge 3

Copy the list using bullet points to separate the items.

Opposites are: this and that, thick and thin, come
and go, here and there.

Sentence types

Challenge 1

Choose a sentence type from the box and write it next to each sentence.

question   exclamation   statement

Fiction books are about storytelling.

Why do we use dictionaries?

I couldn't find my pocket money!

Challenge 2

Sort the words to make a statement and write it out with the correct capital letters and punctuation.

computer my old is not very

like would I a new television

not enough an old ride scooter to electric I am

Copy the sentences, putting in the correct punctuation to make a statement, exclamation or question.

how old are you

he is younger than me

hooray its my birthday

Challenge 3

Copy the passage onto a separate piece of paper putting in the missing punctuation.

My friend farah had invited me to visit the zoo with her. She was a cheerful girl in fact her name meant cheerful it must be hard to have a name like that when you werent feeling cheerful What shall we see first Farah asked.

i thought it would be interesting to see the big cats – the lions tigers leopards and panthers. We walked to the big cats enclosure. The lions looked hungry I expect they were ready for their next meal

look at that one exclaimed farah. Its watching us and licking its lips.

We moved on quickly no one wants to be a big cats next meal

an or a?

Challenge 1

Circle all the words beginning with a vowel sound.

tin   airplane   exit   mouse   ink

lemon   opera   heart   ugly   pan

Write the words that begin with a vowel sound in alphabetical order. Add **an** in front of the words.

Challenge 2

Write **an** or **a** in the sentences then copy them out.

_____ tortoise is _____ unusual pet.

I had _____ aunt who owned one.

She gave it _____ carrot every day.

It lived _____ long time.

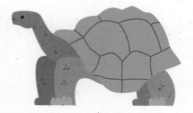

86

Copy the instructions in the correct order onto a separate piece of paper.

How to boil an egg

Get a large spoon and take the egg out of the pan and place it in an egg cup.

Place your egg in the pan.

Time your egg from the moment the water starts to boil.

Put the pan on the cooking ring and turn it on or ask an adult to help.

Enjoy your boiled egg.

Get a pan and fill it with enough cold water to cover an egg.

3 or 4 minutes for a soft-boiled egg and about 8 minutes for a hard-boiled egg.

When your egg is cooked, turn off the cooking ring.

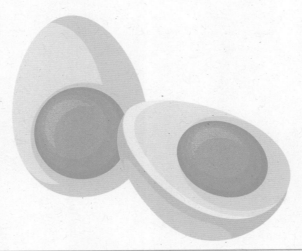

Revising direct speech

Challenge 1

Copy the sentences, putting in the capital letters and correct punctuation.

oh that's my favourite cake she exclaimed

no she yelled don't tip it over

blow out the candles said uncle phil

Challenge 2

Put speech marks in the following conversation. Copy the full conversation.

would you like to come to my house said Alia
oh yes replied maia I haven't been to your
house lets go now squealed Alia.

Challenge 3

Copy the conversation carefully onto a separate piece of paper. Make sure your punctuation is correctly placed and spaced. Fill in the missing words using the words in the box.

asked	forward	said	could
responded	replied	going	

"_____ you get my coat?" _____ Sadie.

"You always forget your scarf; shall I get that too?" _____ Budi.

"I know, I'm very forgetful," _____ Sadie.

"Now you're ready, let's get _____ or we'll be late," Budi said.

"Lead on! I'm looking _____ to seeing our friends when we get to our destination," Sadie _____.

Your neatest writing

Challenge 1

Use the words in the box to complete the sentences and then copy them out in your neatest writing.

touch	occasions	neatest

There are some _____ when you need to write neatly.

When you send a card you use your _____ handwriting.

Handwriting adds a personal _____ to a message.

Challenge 2

Copy the sentences in the correct order and in your neatest writing.

Your grade for the Adventurer test was a pass.

Congratulations on your success!

You are now a qualified Adventurer.

I am writing to tell you your grade.

Dear Sally

Thank you for entering the Adventurers

contest.

Challenge 3

Copy the poem in your neatest handwriting onto a separate piece of paper.

Turkeys don't like Christmas,

Which may come as no surprise.

They say why don't human beings

Pick on people their own size.

To sit beside potatoes

In an oven can't be fun,

So a Turkey is quite justified

To feel he's being done.

'The Turkey' by Richard Digance

1. Copy the words and phrases as quickly and carefully as you can.

| Tip | Remember to space your punctuation marks carefully and clearly. |

"AA stands for Automobile Association," said the mechanic at the garage.

An MP is a Member of Parliament.

"Please, please save some cake for me," begged Dad.

2. Copy the sentences, making sure you put in the commas and bullet points where needed.

I'd like you to buy me some perfume lipstick deodorant and toothpaste

For tomorrow we need: birthday cake sandwiches sausage rolls

3. Copy the sentences quickly and neatly, putting in any speech marks and other punctuation marks that are needed.

Mary please close the door said her dad

The children were tired after their long day at the sports centre where they canoed swam abseiled and cooked their dinner over a log fire

4. Copy the words carefully, thinking about how you join the letters and what height they need to be.

especially   government

interfere   symbol

bruising   theatre

dramatic   janitor

How I feel about...	😐	🙂	😃
placing speech marks around direct speech			
using bullet points			
my quick, legible writing			

Progress check 4

5. Write the contractions of these words.

did not   is not

who have   you are

you will   have not

shall not   she is

6. Copy the words in the correct alphabetical order to the second letter.

major   main   supply   sheep   shepherd

clever   category   vegetable   variety

7. Label each part of the house.

| door | window | roof | chimney | garage |

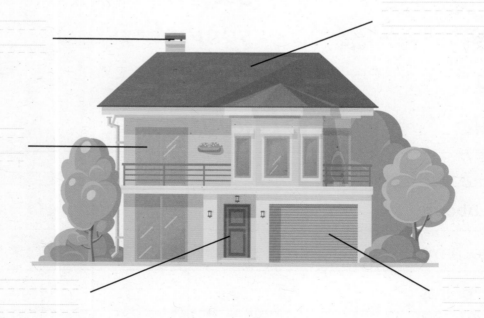

8. Quickly write as many words as you can describing a sunny day – spend no more than 40 seconds.

Complete: I wrote _____ words that could easily be read in 40 seconds.

How I feel about...	😐	🙂	😃
printing and labelling			
contractions			

Progress chart

Draw ticks in the boxes to show how you feel about your handwriting.

	Not sure	Working on it	I can do it!
Joining diagonals			
My ascenders			
My descenders			
Spacing punctuation			
Writing quickly			
Alphabetical order			
Joining to and from the letter **f**			
Joining to and from the letter **t**			
My horizontal joins			
Spacing punctuation			
Punctuating lists			
Alphabetical order to the second letter			
Using contractions			
Using speech marks			
My legible writing			
Writing quick notes			
Printing and labelling			
Placing speech marks around direct speech			
Using bullet points			
My quick, legible writing			